The Sun *and* Moon

Patrick Moore

Illustrated by Paul Doherty

COPPER BEECH BOOKS
BROOKFIELD, CONNECTICUT

Copyright © 1994 Aladdin Books Limited
Text copyright © 1994 by Patrick Moore

Produced by
Aladdin Books Limited
28 Percy Street
London W1P 9FF
Designed by David West Children's Book Design

First published 1994 in the United Kingdom by
Riverswift, Random House, London

First published 1995 in the United States by
Copper Beech Books
an imprint of
The Millbrook Press
2 Old New Milford Road
Brookfield, Connecticut 06804

3 5 4 2

Illustrations by Paul Doherty
Additional illustrations by Mike Lacey and Ian Thompson
Photocredits: Page 6: Science Photo Library; page 18: Melies (Courtesy Kobal
Collection); page 22: Frank Spooner Pictures

Library of Congress Cataloging-in-Publication Data
Moore, Patrick.
The sun and moon / By Patrick Moore: illustrated by Paul Doherty.
p. cm. – (The starry sky)
Includes index
ISBN 1-56294-622-6 (lib. bdg.) 1-56294-640-4 (pbk.)
1. Sun–Juvenile literature. 2. Moon–Juvenile literature. [1. Sun. 2. Moon.]
I. Doherty, Paul, ill. II. Title. III. Series.
QB521.5.M67 1995
523.7–dc20   94-43932
CIP   AC

*My grateful thanks are due to Paul Doherty for his splendid pictures, and to
Lynn Lockett for all her help and encouragement.*
P.M.

Contents

Sometimes you can see the moon in the daytime sky.

The sun and moon in the sky

When it is daytime, and the sky is clear, you can see the sun. At night you can often see the moon. But do you know what the sun and the moon are really like? The sun is much the bigger of the two, but the moon is much closer to us. The Earth on which we live is a planet, shaped like a ball; it moves around the sun, taking a year to go around once. The moon moves around the Earth, taking just over 27 days to do so.

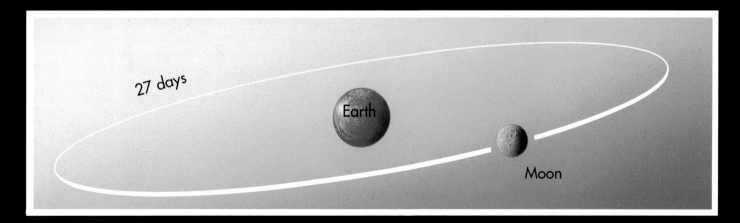

27 days

Earth

Moon

The moon has no light of its own, and shines only because it is being lit up by the sun.

Looking at the sun and moon

The sun is very hot. If you hold out your hand to the sun, you will feel the heat. The sun is also very bright. You must never look straight at the sun. Astronomers use solar telescopes which reflect an image of the sun. The moon sends us almost no heat. You can look straight at the moon for as long as you like and you will not hurt your eyes.

Here an astronomer is measuring the sizes and positions of sunspots, using a very large telescope. Even then, the astronomer must wear dark glasses to make sure that he does not hurt his eyes.

Heat from the sun is so strong that it can quickly burn your skin.

How the sun moves

The Earth turns around once every 24 hours, so that the sky seems to move around from east to west – taking the sun, the moon and the stars with it. This is why the sun seems to rise in the east and set in the west every day.

Summer sun

The sun is higher in the sky in summer than in winter, which is why the days in summer are so warm. When the sun is low down in the sky, its light comes to us through a thicker part of the Earth's air. This makes the sun look orange or red. Even then you must never look straight at it. Do not forget this; you must not hurt your eyes.

Winter sun

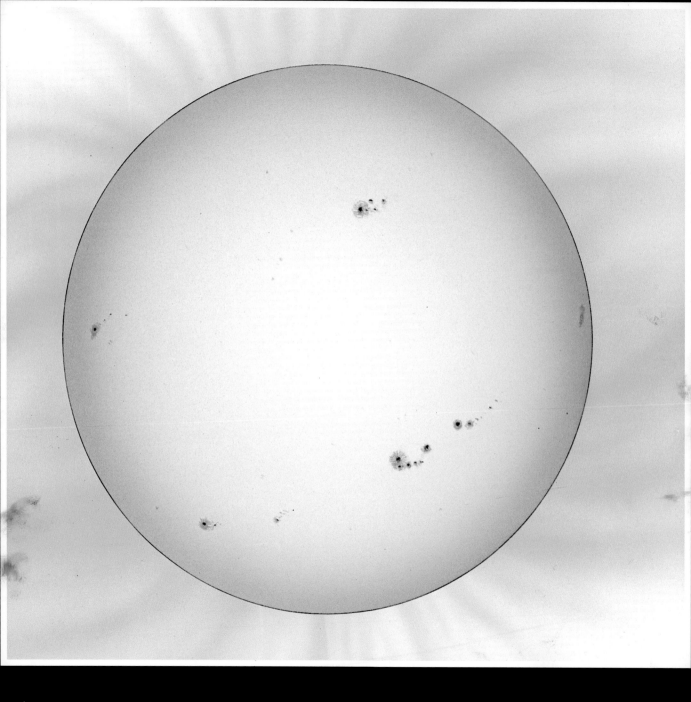

Dark 'sunspots' are cooler patches in the sun's hot gas.

Spots on the sun

The sun is much, much bigger than the Earth. It is not solid, but is made up of gas, so you could not go there even if it were not so hot! Like the Earth, it is spinning around, but it takes nearly four weeks to make one full turn instead of only 24 hours. Sometimes there are dark patches on the sun. These patches are called sunspots. They look black because they are not so hot as the gas around them. They do not last for more than a few days or a few weeks, and at times there may be no sunspots at all.

The sun's heat is much weaker at the Earth's poles, so that the climate there is cold.

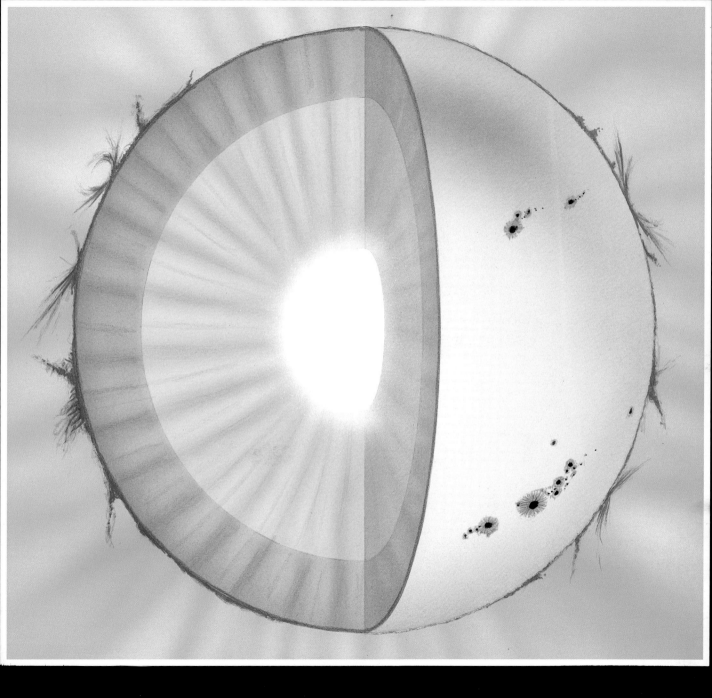

The sun is much hotter inside than it is at its surface.

Hide and seek

Sometimes the sun, the moon and the

Earth move into a straight line, with the

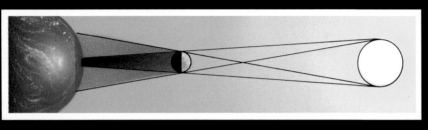

moon in the middle. When this happens,

the moon hides the sun for a short time.

That is what we call an

eclipse.

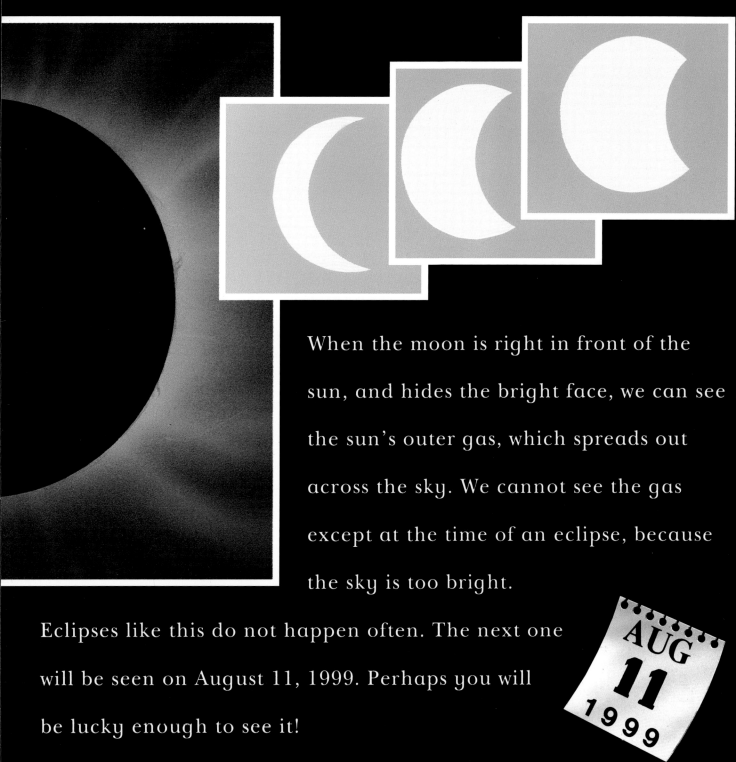

When the moon is right in front of the sun, and hides the bright face, we can see the sun's outer gas, which spreads out across the sky. We cannot see the gas except at the time of an eclipse, because the sky is too bright.

Eclipses like this do not happen often. The next one will be seen on August 11, 1999. Perhaps you will be lucky enough to see it!

AUG
11
1999

How the moon moves

The sun can shine on only half of the moon at once, so that one half of the moon is bright and the other half is dark. This is why the moon seems to change shape. When the moon is almost between the Earth and the sun, its dark side is turned towards us, and we cannot see the moon at all; this is called new moon.

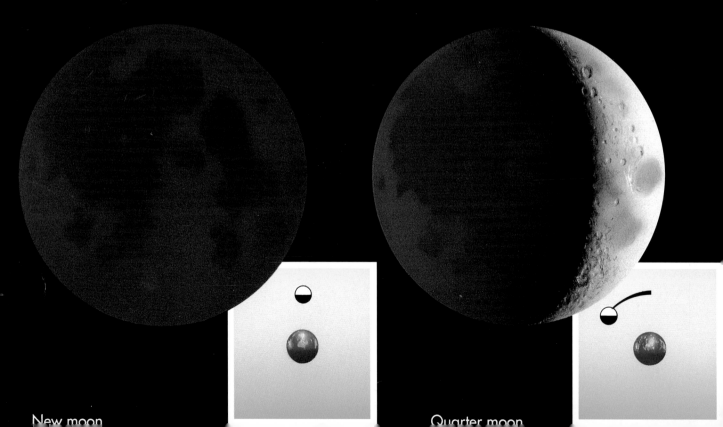

New moon

Quarter moon

As the moon moves in its path, we begin to see a little of the bright side; then we see half of the bright side, and at full moon the whole bright side faces us. Because the moon takes just over 27 days to go once around the Earth, we usually see one new moon and one full moon in every month.

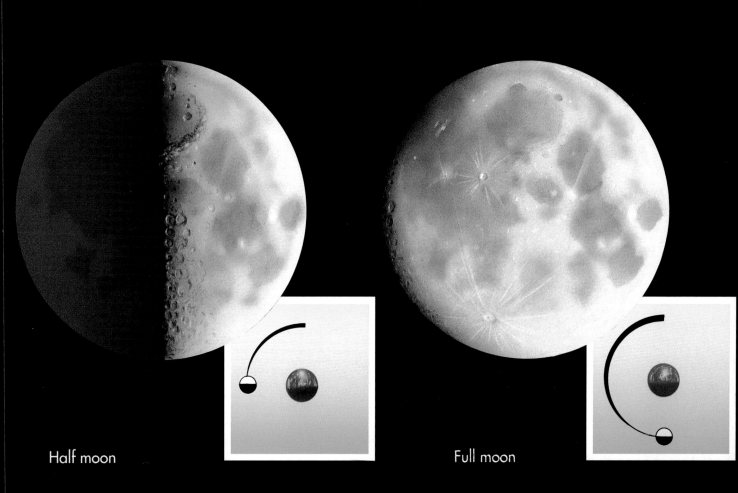

Half moon

Full moon

The face of the moon

When you look at the moon, you can see bright and dark patches. The dark patches are called seas, but they are not real seas; there is no water in them – and in fact there is no water anywhere on the moon. There are high mountains, and there are many craters, which are really holes with walls around them.

The moon's rocky surface

Some people say that the dark patches look rather like a human face – you may have heard of the Man in the Moon. But there are no men on the moon, because there is no air, and without air no one can breathe.

The 'seas' on the moon are low-lying plains.

A view of the Earth as it appears from the moon.

On the moon

If you could go to the moon, you would find that the sky is black even in the daytime. Because there is no air, there are no clouds and no wind; of course it never rains on the moon. The days are much longer than ours.

From the moon you would be able to see the sun and the stars. You would also see the Earth, which would look much bigger and brighter than the moon does to us. Sometimes the Earth would be new, sometimes half and sometimes full, just as we see the moon.

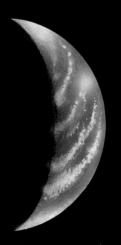

Going to the moon

There is no air between the Earth and the moon, so that you cannot fly there in the same way as you can fly from New York to London. Twelve men have been to the moon, but they went there in rockets instead of aircraft. When you are on the moon, you cannot go outside your rocket without putting on a spacesuit, because there is no air for

Neil Armstrong was the first man on the moon.

you to breathe. But before long we may have the right stations there, and it is possible that you will be able to visit one day.

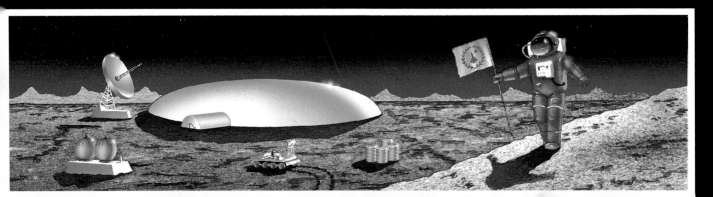

The flag does not wave about, as it would do on Earth, because there is no air on the moon.

Index

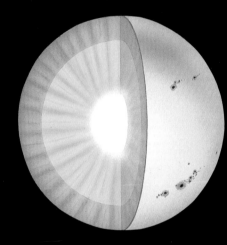
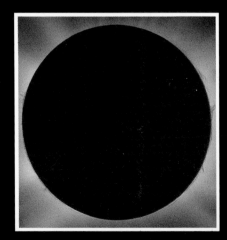